TESTIMONIALS

My review isn't objective because I have, throughout my seventy years, been committed to self-improvement. In sum, gumption and its wise words have been the air I breathe. I have continually been willing to take a hard look at my life and make adjustments as warranted. I've tried to be objective, open to criticism, and willing to learn from those who have traveled the road of life before me. I respect their judgements, their admonishments, and vision for how best to live a life of service. In short, I seek the inspiration of others while valuing my own experiences and beliefs.

My preaching professor, Dr. Bryant Kirkland, offered his fledgling flock of soon-to-be pastors this advice: integrity trumps. *Gumption* is a book that will guide you toward living a life of integrity. You will want to have it nearby, serving as a continual reminder to accept responsibility for your actions, set aside excuses, and strive to be the best person you can be.

—**Rev. Dr. Michael S. Barry,** Author, *The Forgiveness Project*

"Kenneth O'Neal shares his experiences and beliefs in this manifesto aptly titled Gumption. This is a book to inspire and edify.

He combines his own personal journey with theories and beliefs and the result is a book that gives practical advice and points to time worn truths."

—**Kathleen Hudson,** PhD Professor of English,
Schreiner University Kerrville, Texas 1985 to present.
Technical Writing Director of the Freshman Experience
2010 Minnie Piper Stevens Award for Excellence

• • •

"What a wonderful book! Being from the South, I love the word "Gumption" and I love the contents of this book. Anyone who wants to be more successful will benefit from this book!"

—**Howard Partridge**, International Business Coach,
Best-Selling Author

• • •

"I have known Kenneth professionally for more than twenty-five years. His life experiences as a Certified Public Accountant, an entrepreneur, coach and business consultant benefit others. If you feel like you are in a rut or just want to move to a higher level, his advice, knowledge, hope and encouragement go a long way, leading to a meaningful life."

—**Don White**, Certified Public Accountant White
and Associates, CPAS Houston, Texas

• • •

THE CIRCLE OF GUMPTION

THE CIRCLE OF GUMPTION

FROM A TRANSACTION LIFE TO A TRANSFORMED LIFE

KENNETH ROBERT O'NEAL

FOREWORD BY TOM ZIGLAR

ISBN Softcover: 978-1-949550-76-4
ISBN Hardcover: 978-1-949550-78-8
Ebook ISBN: 978-1-949550-79-5

Printed in the United States of America.

Throne Publishing Group
1601 East 69th St N Suite 306
Sioux Falls, SD 57108
ThronePG.com

DEDICATION

To Zig Ziglar, for challenging, teaching, mentoring, and showing me, not only how a true man of God with gumption lives, but how to lead others in and to a well-balanced life.

The example you set changed my life.

From you, I received a wealth of knowledge in attitude and a rich philosophy and culture of life that now enables me to share with others.

I am forever filled with gratitude.

FOREWORD

Have you felt stuck? Is there something you know you want to accomplish but you just keep putting it off? Gumption might be just the thing you need. Gumption is more than just good thinking—it is good doing. Gumption doesn't wait. Instead, regardless of the circumstances, gumption takes action. Kenneth O'Neal has plenty of gumption, and through this book, he shares his with you!

Getting started is not as complicated as we sometimes make it. I heard my dad say many times that we can't take the second step until we take the first step. This book is a great first step. It focuses on the relationships, integrity, trust, love, respect, and gratitude we need as the foundation in our lives.

When you build the right foundation, it solidifies your beliefs, and the depth of your beliefs determines the height of your potential. When you have the right foundation, you can build a life that can weather the storm and make a positive difference in the lives of others.

Gumption is about taking action, and this book is filled with practical examples and steps you can take to not only build the right foundation but to also improve your communication skills, so you can have more fulfilling relationships in every area of your life. Are you ready to get unstuck? Are you ready to build a solid foundation for your life? Are you ready to take the next step? Don't just read this book. Take wise action on what you learn from it!

Tom Ziglar, CEO
Ziglar Corporation and
proud son of Zig Ziglar

TABLE OF CONTENTS

SECTION 1
THE PILLARS IN ACTION

SECTION 2

EFFECTIVE COMMUNICATION

SECTION 3

THE COMMON THREAD

SECTION 4
THE JOURNEY TO GUMPTION

INTRODUCTION

"Though thy beginning was small, yet thy latter end should greatly increase."

—Job 8:7 (KJV)

I am not a professional writer. I write as though I am speaking with you. You are my friend, and we are discussing a topic or concern of mutual interest. My goal is to engage with you in order to inspire and equip you to engage to inspire and equip others. I want you to discover how to live the life God created for you. I want you to be the best you.

I tell lots of stories. Some come from my life, but most of them come from the experiences of other people. Stories allow us to travel to other worlds and places. They are vehicles of effective communication. These stories are metaphors, analogies, or parables.

This book, *The Circle of Gumption*, is a message of encouragement and hope during challenging times like this moment in time, a time we will not soon forget. We are in a pandemic together, and I believe these pillars will allow you to become stronger in times like these. Our thinking and attitude are more important today than ever.

The "Black Swan" theory of events is a metaphor describing an unpredictable event that comes as a surprise, has a major effect, and results in severe consequences. These events are extremely rare and have significant impact. Some examples in the United States of America have been World Wars I and II, the events of 9/11, the financial crisis of 2007–2008, and the current coronavirus pandemic. We have all experienced the effects of hurricanes, tornadoes, divorce, and death of loved ones.

At the end of our lives, we will each leave a legacy—one we should be intentional to design. American pastor and author Mark Batterson said, "Inheritance is what you leave to someone. Legacy is what you leave in someone." Legacy prepares those you love to grow through the most difficult challenges of life. Challenges will come, and we simply cannot protect those we love and care about from obstacles they may face. However, we can be prepared and equip those we love to handle whatever challenges they encounter. We can become stronger by growing through the "Black Swan" life events.

Your mindset and attitude mean that, while you do not like what is happening, you understand and believe you are learning, growing, and becoming stronger. My message has always been, and is even more so today, to help people be successful and become better and more capable because of their challenges, trials, and tribulations. The stronger mindset believes that every trial, pressure, and challenge we face makes us stronger. There must be suffering before significance, and pain before promotion.

Living out the stronger mindset is not easy, but there is no downside. The stronger our beliefs, the stronger our faith. The stronger our hope, the more our spirit is lifted and the more we lift the spirits of those around us. These times are tough. I believe we who live out the stronger mindset with gumption have the opportunity to create a meaningful legacy.

When I started on this journey of becoming a person of gumption, I searched for advice to overcome a difficult situation, a way out of the "valley of the shadow of death." I have weathered the following storms of life, which I call The Dastardly D's:

1. Death of loved ones (both parents, a younger brother, and a sister)
2. Divorces (two)
3. Disease and health issues (prostate cancer and COVID-19)
4. Dissolution of assets (company and financial crisis)
5. Disagreements, misunderstandings, and injustice

Somewhere along the journey, I found a bridge that would carry me out of that dark valley and connect me to the success waiting for me on the other side of my pain. I learned we all hold the power of life and death in our hands. The first step toward accepting self-responsibility is recognizing we have choices in life. We need to be the decision-makers and accept responsibility in our lives, including our careers and relationships. Each day we make more than 20,000 decisions. Most of those decisions happen in our subconscious mind. Every day, three or four significant items of urgency and importance will come across our path. We have the power within to choose and intentionally create our lives. We must live an intentional life of gumption.

When you choose to live a life of gumption, your heart will be pure and your path will be clear. You have an opportunity to make a choice and be responsible for your decision.

By crossing that bridge away from the Dastardly D's that made up my "valley of the shadow of death," I had to learn what was required to be the right person and do the right things, so I could give to others and create a legacy to last through eternity. I call these lessons "The Four Pillars of Gumption," as they uphold all that it means to be a person of gumption. These four pillars are intended to challenge you to reflect on your thoughts, feelings, mindset, and perceptions:

Pillar 1: The Pillar of Being
Pillar 2: The Pillar of Doing
Pillar 3: The Pillar of Giving
Pillar 4: The Pillar of Legacy

I have read, researched, studied, lived, and organized the principles behind these pillars in all my life experiences as: a United States Air Force veteran, a certified public accountant, a father of four, a husband of two, a Rotarian, a Toastmaster, a mediator, an academy preparatory school staff member, an advisory board member of the local Salvation Army KROC, a business owner and consultant, a nationwide instructor for accounting, tax and securities seminars, and a Zig Ziglar licensed certified coach and trainer.

American author and motivational speaker Zig Ziglar was a person of gumption who helped further my understanding of the attributes of these four pillars when he said, "Man was designed for accomplishment, engineered for success and endowed with the seeds of greatness." Now, I hope to help you understand these pillars and obtain these attributes, too.

As you continue to read this book, the principles taught here will give you the tools to achieve your purpose in life and will begin as gnosis, or "head knowledge," which is simply digested knowledge based on personal experience or perception. With time and positive actions, your understanding of these four pillars will move from "head knowledge" to "heart knowledge," or epignosis. These pillars will become your closest allies—reliable and ready to assist you during challenges. You will obtain true wealth, which is much more than material assets. Your ambitions and desires will transform into true success, in which you use your talents and skills to honor your Creator at the highest level.

Have you lived a life of tears without feeling the great power of love? Has the true meaning of life been elusive to you? Have you had many wasted years? Have you lived in darkness and fear, drifting aimlessly through the days, weeks, and years? Have you experienced challenges in life and are now ready to accept responsibility and be held accountable for your actions? If you answered *yes* to any of these questions, then I dedicate *The Circle of Gumption* to you! It is my desire that you learn and discover your priceless personal skills and talents while you have more productive years ahead of you than behind you. Do not live a life of regrets.

I believe God is calling you to turn around from a life of wasted years. God is listening and hearing you. Give up the burden you carry. God and I want you to enjoy a life of happiness, excellent health, a certain amount of prosperity, a feeling of security and safety, peace and contentment, hope for the future, and high-level winning relationships with God, your family, and especially with yourself. *The Circle of Gumption* will speak to your mind, soul, and heart. May you live a life of being the right person, doing the right things, having all the abundance of this life, giving and serving others, and creating a legacy for eternity.

"No discipline seems pleasant at the time, but painful. Later on, however, it produces a harvest of righteousness and peace for those who have been trained by it."

—(Hebrews 12:11 NIV)

PROLOGUE: DEFINING GUMPTION

WHAT IS GUMPTION?

"Gumption is a word for common sense ... but common sense is no longer common."

—Annie Reynolds (my grandmother)

In the 1950s and 1960s, my grandmother told me "Gumption is a word for common sense." Then she would always add, "Common sense is no longer common." Her conversations would include statements like, "Use your gumption" or "He has no gumption." The best was when she was exasperated with me for a wrongdoing and would ask, "Kenneth, where is your gumption?" We could use more gumption and common sense in the world. Sadly, gumption is no longer common, and neither is common sense.

Gumption is an old Scottish word used sparingly in the modern world. It refers to a culture of no-nonsense effective communication with the spirit of excellence. The word originated in 1719 to mean common sense, shrewdness, and acuteness of practical understanding. It also meant drive and initiative, possibly connected to the Middle English word "gome" and from the Old Norse word "gaumr," both meaning heed and attention. In English, the word "heed" means to pay attention to and take notice. First recorded in 1812, the English word "attention" means the action of dealing with or taking special care of someone or something. The related word "gumptious" is an adjective, its usage providing clear evidence of the word from 1823.

A person of gumption knows who they are, and, because of it, they know what to do.
They are self-aware and always at the forefront of listening, learning, leading, and watching to see what is just ahead and meeting it head-on with gusto. A person with gumption has cast away all transgressions and has a new heart and spirit. They are servants to others and always speak the truth. Gumption does not come naturally.

So how does one go from living a mundane life to one of gumption?
When you obtain and live a life of gumption, your heart will be pure and your path will be clear. You have an opportunity to make a choice and be responsible for your decision to be, to do, to give, and to create a legacy. These choices make up the Four

Pillars of Gumption, and the framework for these pillars exists within effective communication. The lives of all those brought into your life by God will live on through eternity when you do your very best to serve them at a high level of loving-kindness.

The Circle of Gumption is the reflection of eternity.
There is no beginning; there is no ending.
There is no division.
There is love erasing a sense of time,
Eliminating memories of beginning and ending.

THE PILLARS IN ACTION

CARING FOR OTHERS

"No one cares how much you know, until they know how much you care."

—Theodore Roosevelt

Especially in these turbulent times, lost souls are everywhere—some are in hospitals, some in prison, some in drug and alcohol rehabilitation, and some are simply confused, uncertain of their future, and fearful. The following stories are examples of ordinary people showing extraordinary gumption. As you read, see if you can identify the four pillars in action.

THE GENOCIDE IN RWANDA

Although born in Rwanda, Paul Kagame, its current president, grew up in exile in Uganda. His parents fled Rwanda when he was a young child in 1959, when Hutu violence toward the Tutsi increased during the buildup to Rwandan independence from Belgium. After studying at Makerere University, he joined the forces of Museveni, who overthrew Ugandan President Obote in 1986. Afterwards, Kagame became the chief of intelligence for Uganda and gained a reputation for incorruption and severity with a stringent code of conduct and behavior.

In the late 1980s, Kagame and three other expatriate Rwandan military leaders organized the Rwandan Patriotic Front (RPF) led by the Tutsis and began to plot an invasion of their homeland. The invasion was defeated by Rwandan forces, and the other three RPF command members were killed. Rwanda faced a great crisis, and, once again, Kagame left Rwanda—this time to regroup and assume direction and control of the civil war. In August 1993, the war was suspended by a promised agreement of power sharing by the warring parties and the United Nations. The general in charge, Lt. General Romeo Dallaire, was sent to Rwanda to help these two warring parties achieve their desired peace.

Unfortunately, the agreement never came to fruition. In January 1994, the Rwandan president, Habyarimana, who was a Hutu, was killed when his plane was shot down by an unknown party. In the one hundred days following this event, approximately 800,000 people were slaughtered in Rwanda by ethnic Hutu extremists targeting members of the minority Tutsi community, as well as their political opponents, irrespective of ethnic origin.

While the typical customary rhetoric is that the genocide was a sudden catastrophe that began with the gunning down of President Habyarimana's airplane, Lt. General Dallaire made it very clear that the build-up to the massacre was apparent long before the plane crashed. When Lt. General Dallaire arrived in Rwanda, he and members of his small international force found themselves caught up in a vortex of civil war and genocide.

Under the indictment of the petty bureaucrats who refused to give him the men and freedom of operation to stop the killing, Lt. General Dallaire left Rwanda a broken man with disillusions and suicidal thoughts—but also brimming with determination to tell his story. Lt. General Dallaire had issued stark warning of the imminent bloodshed to everyone at the United Nations and leaders around the world. He had pleaded for more troops and supplies. The United Nations ignored his call for help and blocked his attempts to build an effective force. Historical records show the United Nations' failure to hear the plea for aid against the moral cowardice that allowed the genocide in Rwanda. Humanity failed Rwanda.

Keenly aware of the crisis and its magnitude, Kagame returned with his forces in July 1994. With minimal casualties, he was able to take control of the Rwandan capital city of Kigali and set up a government with its new president, Pasteur Bizimungu, a Hutu. However, the real power appeared to be with Kagame, who assumed the titles of vice president and minister of defense. Because of his strengths in communicating and leading, Kagame was elected president of Rwanda by the National Assembly in 2000.

Lt. General Dallaire later stated, "I know there is a God because in Rwanda I shook hands with the devil. I have seen him, I have smelled him and I have touched him. I know the devil exists, and therefore I know there is a God."

As conveyed so eloquently by Lt. General Dallaire in the above statement, I saw firsthand how Rwanda was this unforgettable parable of good and evil during my time and travels there from 2015 to 2016. I found the people of Rwanda, no matter the tribe, to be joyful, forgiving, and loving.

While there, I heard a story of Frederick Ndabaramiye, a small Christian boy with great faith whose hands were amputated when he disobeyed Hutu aggressors. The killers intended the atrocity for harm, but God meant it for good. The young lad was bound by rope at his wrists, which served as a make-shift tourniquet and ultimately saved his life. His disability fueled his passion, his purpose, and his God-given mission to begin the Ubumwe Community Center, where people with disabilities can come to this day to discover their purpose in life. This is a tremendous story of faith, forgiveness, and hope, as well as perseverance and gumption. This story also displays the best of human kindness and the worst of human behavior.

ANOTHER BODY AT BELLEVUE HOSPITAL

It was a routine admission to New York City's Bellevue Hospital on a cold, windy, dreary January morning in 1864. The man struggled for life but was counted as just another drunken bum with a slashed throat from the Bowery. He died soon after and was received at the morgue with his name misspelled on the form. His age was also incorrect—he was thirty-eight, not thirty-nine. Maybe someone thought about how young he was, but nobody actually cared, so nothing was said.

Sometime after, a friend found the man and properly identified him. Among his few personal belongings were thirty-eight cents and a scrap of paper with the following words, "Dear friends and gentle hearts..." Now, if you think that sounds like words to a song, you are correct. In fact, the dead man wrote more than two hundred songs about our rich American heritage, "Oh! Susanna" and "Camptown Races". His name was Stephen Collins Foster, and he was one of our most influential songwriters. Someone, his friend, finally stepped up with love, compassion, and care for a lost soul.

THE GOOD SAMARITAN

One of the most famous Biblical parables told by Jesus Christ is the story of "The Good Samaritan." It is written in the Gospel of Luke 10:27 (NIV) that a certain lawyer stood up and replied to a question from Jesus, "'Love the Lord your God with all your heart and with all your soul and with all your strength and with all your mind' and, 'Love your neighbor as yourself.'" The lawyer continued, "Who is my neighbor?" Then Jesus shared this story:

> A man was going down from Jerusalem to Jericho, when he was attacked by robbers. They stripped him of his clothes, beat him and went away, leaving him half dead. A priest happened to be going down the same road, and when he saw

> the man, he passed by on the other side. So too, a Levite, when he came to the place and saw him, passed by on the other side. But a Samaritan, as he traveled, came where the man was; and when he saw him, he took pity on him. He went to him and bandaged his wounds, pouring on oil and wine. Then he put the man on his own donkey, brought him to an inn and took care of him. The next day he took out two denarii[e] and gave them to the innkeeper. 'Look after him,' he said, 'and when I return, I will reimburse you for any extra expense you may have.' Which of these three do you think was a neighbor to the man who fell into the hands of robbers?" Luke 10:30-36 (NIV)

The lawyer answered that it was the one who had shown the man mercy. Jesus noted the Samaritan was the least likely to help the traveler and had nothing to gain, but his compassion made him the traveler's neighbor.

CARING IN ACTION

What do these three stories all have in common? What do they tell us about gumption?

The military leader, Paul Kagame, the unnamed friend of Stephen Collins Foster, and the Good Samaritan were men of gumption. Driven by a life purpose, each person valued the lives of others and jumped into action. They were kind, concerned about the welfare of the injured party members, and had the maturity level to make proper decisions. These men had the knowledge that gave them power over the situations, and they understood the law of sowing and reaping. They gave of themselves unconditionally, expecting nothing in return. Each one created a better situation by being the best of mankind.

Everything that has been done in the world's history has been completed by someone—somebody who took control of their thoughts, words, and deeds and exercised their power over a situation. Their share of the responsibility depended on their environment and social structure. Our responsibility increases with maturity.

Adam and Eve had charge over the Garden of Eden. When Adam ate the apple, he pointed the finger at Eve and laid the responsibility on her. She turned around and said the snake was responsible. Adam and Eve were irresponsible and failed in completing their call to action. Responsiblity means having an obligation or dury to perform, having control over a project or caring for someone. Synonyms include: authority, importance, power, liability, or obligation. Responsibility is a sign of maturity. A person of gumption responds to a call of action to be held accountable.

People with gumption are mature and have taken charge of their lives and their conduct. They own their actions and answer for them.

Until you take control and responsibility for your life, someone else controls it. Stand up, be accountable, answer the call to action, take control of the situation, and see it through to completion. Be a person of gumption.

Do you care enough to be hospitable, kind, and considerate? Will you listen and learn from the stories of these three men?

"What is man, that thou art mindful of him?"

—Psalms 8:4a (KJV)

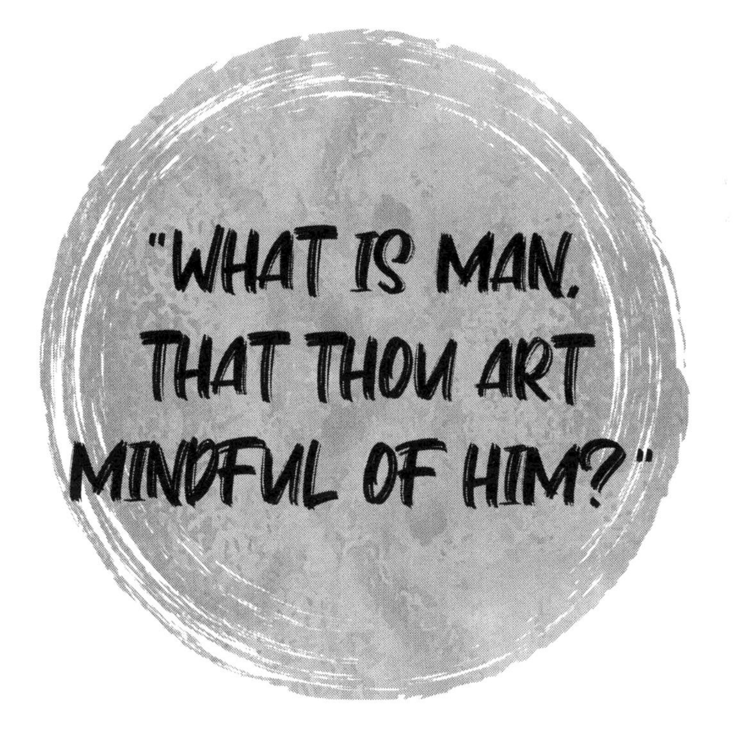

- PSALMS 8:4A (KJV)

EFFECTIVE COMMUNICATION

HEALTHY COMMUNICATION

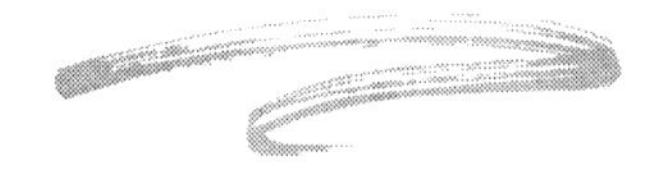

"Well, it's really no use our talking in the way we have been doing if the words we use mean something different to each of us ... and nothing."

—Malcolm Bradbury, Eating People is Wrong

With effective communication, relationships are formed, and good relationships can be made extraordinary. Effective communication is not easy, but it is worth the effort, as relationships, productivity, and bottom line results are all improved. Effective communication can even save a life during tragedy.

LEADERSHIP

How can a newly graduated West Point lieutenant lead a platoon of fifty men and women into battle? It takes gumption and effective communication, which requires two or more people making verbal and nonverbal contact amidst everyday life situations. Officers with gumption are determined and full of courage, with common sense. They do not give up. They have the confidence to get difficult things done. They are fearless and not afraid to take risks.

Leaders must be effective communicators. The most important job of a military leader is to create a positive atmosphere to energize, give hope, and encourage the troops with connected relationships and great teamwork. They must inspire and equip them to learn and grow in becoming their very best. Hope and encouragement create a belief system that determines habits that create the future.

In contrast, when we ignore people, we participate in a form of negative communication. Officer leaders must not allow their bias and pre-conceived ideas to permeate (or color or influence) their adult-to-adult conversations. These barriers to communication can be lifted by bonding and creating rapport with the new troops to establish trust. The new lieutenant must have empathy by letting the troops know he or she has walked in their shoes.

Communication occurs whenever two or more people make verbal and nonverbal contact during everyday life situations. Effective communicators are empowered with leadership and communication skills, resulting in greater self-confidence and personal growth. Their individual values are respect, integrity, service, and excellence. Their commitment to self-development goes beyond themselves. They are sincerely interested in the welfare of their people and create a high level of trust up front. Effective communication fosters healthy, winning relationships where we are kind to each other, listen at an empathetic level, and tell the truth. Winning relationships bring enormous joy to life by generating respect, understanding, and appreciation, which is priceless and drastically needed in the midst of human interaction.

WORDS, TONALITY, AND BODY LANGUAGE

Effective communication is the proper mutual exchange of thoughts, messages, beliefs, feelings, goals, values, facts, or information. The keyword is exchange.

You can think of effective communication as a formula for the message's quality plus the quality of delivery minus any interference.

(Message Quality + Delivery Quality) – Interference = Communication Effectiveness

You can control what you say, how you say it, your body language, and how you act when you communicate. American author and businessman Stephen Covey said, "Most people do not listen with the intent to understand; they listen with the intent to reply." Think of a good conversation as a two-step process: after the other person speaks, first think and reflect on what you heard. Then, respond rather than react. Effective communication is a like a contact sport and should be full of emotion with three parts:

Words

Men speak approximately twelve thousand words on an average day while, on the same day, women speak approximately twenty-five thousand words. There is an old joke that states, "Women have to repeat everything because men have selective listening and hearing." In a normal conversation, men and women speak about one hundred and fifty to two hundred words each minute, but our minds think at six hundred to seven hundred words a minute. When considering these figures, you can begin to see some of the problems faced with having effective communication.

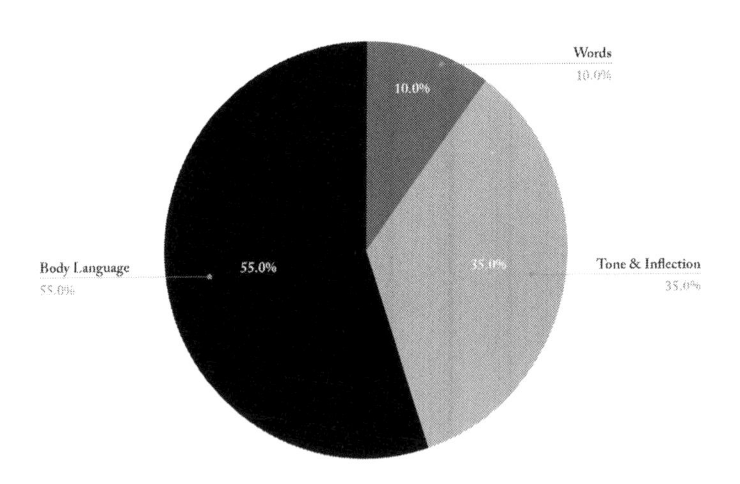

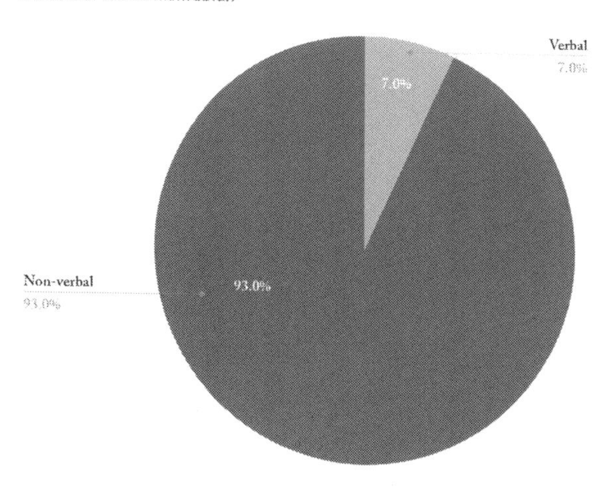

Words, by themselves, are powerful and very important as they can inspire or discourage your audience. They must always be selected with care. Words are critical and account for 8 to 10 percent of effective communication.

English is a very complicated language. For example, there is no egg in "eggplant." There is no ham in "hamburger." There is no pine or apple in "pineapple." We park on driveways, and we drive on parkways. A stand-alone word is not enough to relay the full exchange of information at an ideal level of communication. In the English language, we use approximately five hundred words that have more than fourteen thousand different meanings. As an example, look at the spelling, pronunciation, and meaning of these simple words that all sound the same, but have very different meanings.

SALE | SAIL

In the past several years, I have worked with a small group of women ages eighteen to forty-five in a rehabilitation halfway house for minor crimes, including drug and alcohol abuse. One day, I was teaching and speaking on the impact of words when I mentioned the word, "bond." A young woman from the back of the room commented, "I made my bail bond yesterday." After the laughter subsided, I clarified my meaning to the group. I was thinking more about an investment bond or the bonding and rapport within a winning relationship.

Tone and Inflection

Tone and inflection account for approximately 35 percent of effective communication. It is vital you understand the power of your voice, as the meaning of your words is based upon tonality or inflection. This can happen with only one word. The meaning of a word can be changed by focusing on a single truth, "Not what you said, but how you said it." A misplaced comma can entirely change the meaning of a sentence. For example, notice the placement of the comma in these two short sentences: "Let's eat Mom" or "Let's eat, Mom." Even a slight shift in pitch or pattern could easily lead to miscommunication or even a complete change in message.

Body Language

Body language accounts for approximately 55 percent of effective communication and can be defined as nonverbal, physical behavior expressing or conveying information. It can include space, facial expressions, body posture, hand gestures, touch, and eye movement. Professor Albert Mehrabian, Professor Emeritus of Psychology at the University of California, Los Angeles, takes this even further. It is his contention that 93 percent of communication is nonverbal and only 7 percent verbal. The major reason for the importance of body language is that there are twenty-two times more nerve endings from the eye to the brain than from the ear to the brain, which is likely why 60 percent of individuals are visual learners. Visual impressions are powerful, so strong nonverbal communication skills are very important. It takes words, tonality, and inflection to have effective communication on a higher adult-to-adult level.

Negative Body Language

Nonverbal cues can discredit your influence. The four most common types of negative communication are:

- Aggressive: invades your space, overly squeezes your hand while shaking, points their finger at you like stabbing, places hands on their hips, and stares with eye contact
- Defensive: makes little eye contact, crosses arms, and leans away from you with hunched shoulders
- Nervous: has weak handshake, fidgets, coughs, nail bites, and places hands on their heads
- Bored: makes no eye contact, yawns at every breath, excessively fidgets with rubbing face, and shifts weight constantly.

Positive Body Language

Positive body language stems from nonverbal movements that communicate interest and energy in the topic of discussion. A positive person is relaxed, engaged in the conversation, and makes good eye contact. They have a confident posture with positive gestures like nodding in agreement and smiling in concurrence. They come across as being at ease and very comfortable. In a good conversation with positive body language, everyone is given their opportunity to speak, and no one person ever dominates the conversation.

Body language cannot be learned overnight. It takes time and practice to be natural and genuinely open, confident, and engaged. Awareness, purpose, and energy, along with a great smile, are needed to master the art of body language. Body language can be improved by being relaxed, in an open posture. I sometimes call this the perfect athletic position, balanced on the balls of the feet with legs spread, evenly balanced. You should maintain good eye contact to appear confident and hold the gaze for only a few seconds.

"The most important thing in communication is hearing what isn't said."

—Peter Drucker

LISTENING

Active listening is an integral part of outstanding relationships created and bound by effective communication. Listening is defined as receiving language through the ears and involves

"THE MOST IMPORTANT THING IN COMMUNICATION IS HEARING WHAT ISN'T SAID."

- PETER DRUCKER

identifying the sounds of speech and processing them into words and sentences. Listening is the first of the four language skills. The other three are speaking, reading, and writing. In listening, we use our ears to receive individual sounds, and we use our brain to convert these sounds into messages meaning something to us. Listening in any language requires focus and attention. It is a learned skill and is usually the first language skill learned. Some people need to work more than others on this skill. We learn this skill by interacting with people who already know how to speak the language. For effective communication to occur, you must be an active listener.

There are five levels of listening:

1. Pretend—This is the lowest level of listening. People listen to the words, but are not paying attention. This is rude and a waste of time for the speaker and the feigning listener.
2. Selective—People listen to the words, but only hear what they want to hear. People at this level are not open to learning new things.
3. Content—These people are only interested in hearing the facts. They usually interpret the information without asking questions and obtaining clarity. Miscommunication occurs with this type of listening.
4. Empathetic—These people listen from the other person's point of view. This helps the speaker feel they are being understood in their presentation of facts, which creates a situation of reciprocity. Each party understands

not only the content of the information, but the intent. Sincere interest creates trust, appreciation, and respect.

5. Synergistic—This is the highest level of listening and focuses on alignment and congruence. It leads to learning at higher levels, creating opportunities for collaboration. People keep an open mind to new possibilities, novel ideas, and unexpected suggestions. To work effectively, the communication must occur in an environment of mutual trust where the communicators feel free to express unusual or creative ideas without ridicule or criticism. This level of listening is an important tool for business, as it can be a great source of innovation and of finding new and potentially more efficient ways of working. The communication should not be aimless, but managers and staff need to be willing to abandon their attachment to entrenched processes and idealogies and be prepared to explore better ways of doing things.

Empathetic and synergistic listening are tough to do with only your ears. For these types of listening to occur, there must be an emotional connection, so you must also use your heart to get to these levels. The most productive benefits in business and personal life come from the empathetic and synergistic listening levels.

While these types of listening take practice, oftentimes they occur naturally. An example of this is how many Americans crave an emotional connection with the president of the United States. Looking back, we can identify this type of connection with Ronald Reagan in 1984 and with George H.W. Bush in 1988.

At the 1988 Bush and Dukakis debate, coming out of the National Convention, Dukakis was ahead of Bush by seventeen points. During the debate, CNN's Bernard Shaw asked a disgustingly graphic hypothetical question about Dukakis's wife, Kitty, being raped and murdered, with the death penalty question thrown in. Dukakis was against the death penalty and had said so on many occasions in the past. Dukakis did not believe the death penalty was a deterrent to crime. His answer came across negatively, as a real cold fish with no emotion. Dukakis looked weak, unemotional, uninvolved, and unpresidential as he buried his emotions.

Dukakis and his people missed the boat. They failed to understand that communication is a contact sport. They failed to reach the hearts and minds of their listeners. They failed to reach the emotional part of the audience's mind. They needed to make an emotional contact with their audience, the people of America. Dukakis sealed off his emotional responses and could not establish a connection to move the country.

"Most of the successful people I've known are the ones who do more listening than talking."

—Bernard Baruch

"MOST OF THE SUCCESSFUL PEOPLE I HAVE KNOWN ARE THE ONES WHO LISTEN MORE THAN THEY TALK."

- BERNARD BARUCH

Barriers to Effective Communication

"The superior man blames himself.
The inferior man blames others."

—Don Shula

In the 1980s, I taught accounting at the University of Houston. A professor asked me to teach his class the following night and to "be there at five o'clock to seven o'clock." Upon my arrival at seven o'clock, the students were leaving the classroom. I glanced at one and said, "What is going on?" The student replied,

"Class is over, started at five, over at seven." The biggest miscommunication is to assume communication has taken place.

To show the negative impact of miscommunication, two examples immediately come to mind. The first example is from the famous 1970's movie, *Cool Hand Luke.* In the movie, the warden (played by Strother Martin) always assumes things are the fault of Luke (played by Paul Newman), no matter the circumstances. Luke is not willing to take any of the blame. The warden keeps saying, "What we've got here is failure to communicate. Some men you just can't reach. So, you get what we had here last week, which is the way he wants it. Well, he gets it. I don't like it any more than you men." The warden recognizes the issue, and he still cannot seem to communicate the issue in a way that makes sense.

The second example of miscommunication is from a YouTube clip about a blind man sitting on the street, collecting donations and holding a sign that reads, "I am blind." A lady approaches and changes the words on his cardboard sign to read, "It is a beautiful day and I cannot see it." Before the lady made the change to the message on the man's sign, there were only a few donations in the man's pan. However, after the change was made, the man's donation pan became overflowing with coins and dollars, providing physical proof of the importance of word choice. We participate in a form of negative communication when we ignore people.

The Blame Game

Research over the years shows that many of the interactions between two or more individuals reproduce common relational dysfunctions known as the drama triangle. Most novels, plays, movies, and television series are based on the drama triangle. This behavioral pattern is often very damaging, especially to a purported cohesive team with a common goal such as a marriage. An enormous amount of time and energy is wasted on drama.

The transactional analysis drama triangle has three positions: victim, persecutor, and rescuer. If you find yourself in any of the triangle's positions and stay in the triangle for an extended period, you will become the victim.

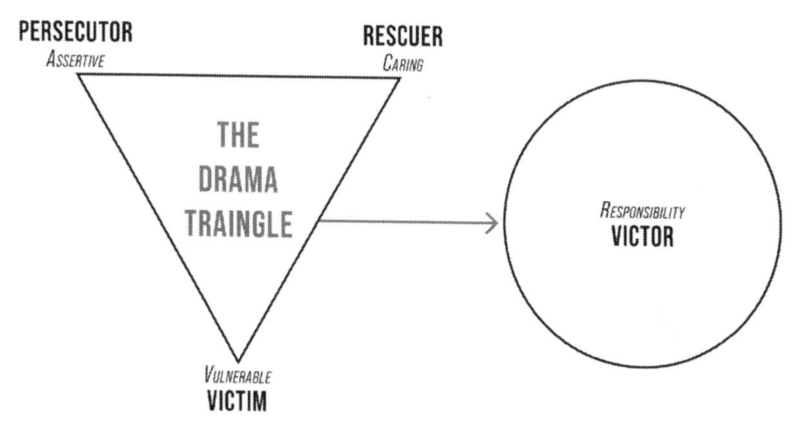

Karpman's Drama Triangle: How We Avoid the Triangle, Get In & Out, July 29th, 2021, https://www.makingbusinessmatter.co.uk/karpmans-drama-triangle/

Who are you in your relationships?

"Poor me" or "It is not my fault," states the victim. They play games such as, "If it were not for ..." or "Woe is me." They play the role of being hopeless, helpless, and powerless. The victim believes other people make them feel good or bad. Victims have a tendency to look for the rescuer to perpetuate their negative feelings and bad attitude.

"What were you thinking?" or "It is all your fault" is the position of the persecutor. They believe they can make you feel bad. They set strict, unnecessary limits, blame, criticize, and keep victims oppressed. They are moved by anger and are rigid in their stance.

"Let me help you," states the rescuer. Often their motivation is pure and rooted in a desire to help, but sometimes the goal of the rescuer is to keep the victim dependent on them.

Once you are in the drama triangle, it can be very difficult to get out. Players begin to shift positions.

You can stay out of or get out of the drama triangle if you are in it by taking on a position outside of it. This position is called responsibility. Ask yourself the following questions: What are my options? What can I learn from this situation? What is my responsibility in this situation? What will I do differently next time?

COMMUNICATION IN ACTION

"Words should be used as tools of communication and not as a substitute for action."

—Mae West, American stage and film actress

GROUND RULES FOR EFFECTIVE COMMUNICATION IN AN ORGANIZATION

- The ideas and concepts presented are heard, and people act upon them correctly, appropriately, and in a timely manner.
- The entire organization must come before any personal ambition or agenda. This can be a team, corporation, self-employed business, family, or church.

RUTH BADER GINSBURG AND ANTONIN SCALIA

Ruth Bader Ginsburg and Antonin Scalia became great friends when they met in the early 1980s while serving in the federal circuit court in Washington, D.C. They were both from New York; she was from Brooklyn, and he was from Queens. She was Jewish, and he was an Italian/Catholic. They both taught law at prestigious universities and were near the same age. He was brash, burley, and conservative, believing in strict adherence to the Constitution in its original text. She was soft spoken and liberal, believing in a living Constitution that can change with the times. Scalia and Ginsburg prided themselves on embracing people for who they were and not how they voted. They had friends from all walks of life, races, creeds, nationalities, sexual orientations, and political persuasions.

Justice Ginsburg, the second woman appointed to the Supreme Court and leading litigator for women's rights in the nation, died September 18, 2020 from complications of metastatic pancreatic cancer. Her time on the United States Supreme Court was monumental and will be assessed for years to come. Justice Scalia died in 2016.

In the early 1980s, when they served in the federal circuit court, ideologically, they were miles apart, with her on the far left and him on the far right. Their individual views were strongly held, but they did not let those very different views weaken or cause the collapse of their deep friendship. It is known that the Ginsburgs and the Scalias celebrated the incoming of each New Year, went souvenir shopping together, and even rode an elephant together in India. They shared a love of opera and excellent wine. When Chief Justice Roberts announced the death of

Justice Ginsburg's husband, Marty, Justice Scalia openly wept from the bench.

While they were opposite in their interpretation of the Constitution, the two justices were good friends during their years together on the U.S. Supreme Court, despite often disagreeing on controversial cases.

There was a time when Justice Scalia delivered flowers to Justice Ginsburg for her birthday and a colleague asked Justice Scalia, "Why do you give her flowers? How many times has she ever sided with you on a 5–4 decision?" Justice Scalia responded without hesitation, "Some things are more important than votes."

I imagine Justices Ginsburg and Scalia as effective communicators and persons of gumption. When in early conversations, they realized mature dialogue required critical, upfront agreements or ground rules between them that clearly explained the relationship's rules. Most people will forget the ground rules and will need to be reminded how the relationship works so it can continue. The justices never had to be reminded because they realized all involved parties had rights and responsibilities. They were sincere in their interest of each other, they listened at a synergistic level, reflecting on the thoughts and discussions, and nurtured the relationship to develop a lasting bond until their deaths. Their values were above reproach. Those values included:

> First, the belief that the law must come before any personal ambition. Second, an honest, truthful openness to the other's opinion on difficult issues, so the focus receives lasting

results. Third, emotional responses must be controlled to obtain full disclosure and complete information. Fourth, make a choice about accountability. Fifth, each member must manage their morale, motivation, and commitment to support all others. There will be no blaming, no condemning, no finger pointing, no criticism, and no complaining. A powerful adult position would be stated as follows: "As I reflect on this situation, I want to acknowledge my contribution to the problem."

THE ART OF A MEDIATOR

I am a mediator, certified to work before the court. Mediation is a process of negotiations in a relationship to resolve differences. Mediating a divorce case involves a couple working with a neutral third party to help them resolve issues of child custody and support and division of assets, liabilities, and property. The judge in the case can mandate the case go to mediation, but the process remains voluntary and parties are not required to come to an agreement. Typically, there are strong relationship barriers to negotiating a solution. The parties distrust each other. Mediation is appropriate when parties are having difficulties resolving a disagreement because of a lack of communication skills and resistance to confronting the opposing party.

Mediators are trained to handle emotional barriers to settlement, problems of misperception, and poor communication. The majority of parties in disputes in relationship, business, and divorce are unwilling to meet face-to-face to discuss the dispute and options. A mutual agreement where the parties maintain control of the outcome and take ownership of the decision is preferable to a third-party judge and jury imposing a decision or verdict. The mediation process can repair or rebuild new working relations critical to ongoing work to be done, especially in the lives of children of divorcing parents. A mediator can end the appeals from both parties and allow a binding agreement to be completed. The mediation can end years of litigation. An assessment and several days of healthy discussion can save an enormous amount of money and keep the court docket from being bogged down with frivolous cases. The mediation guidelines and ground rules are included to display the action steps to a successful mediation.

1. Introduction and welcome to participants, who may be in separate rooms.
2. Definition of mediation is explained as a process under which an impartial person (mediator) facilitates communication between the parties to promote reconciliation, settlement, or understanding among them. The mediator may suggest ways to resolve the dispute, but will not impose judgment on the issues. The mediator is neutral and will not take sides, lecture, provide legal advice, or recommend decisions.
3. The mediator is an advocate for resolution and uses best efforts to assist the parties in reaching a mutually accepted settlement agreement.
4. Both parties must agree to accept the mediator.
5. Principles of mediation are private and informal.
   a. There is no interrupting, no name calling, or talking over the other party.

b. Note taking is recommended.
c. Parties commit individually with best efforts to solve problems and issues.
d. Breaks will be taken as needed.
e. Cell phones, computers, and other electronics are turned off.
f. No weapons are allowed in the meeting rooms.
g. There should be no deadlines or obligation at a specific time before the mediation is completed.
h. Confidential information disclosed by the parties during the course of the mediation will not be divulged unless instructed to do so by the party. All records, reports and other documents received will be held in confidence. The contents of the mediation will not be discussed outside of mediation proceedings. The only record of the mediation will be the date notation of those participants in attendance.
i. The mediation may be held with all parties present in a single meeting room, or, if necessary, in individual meeting rooms. The mediator will go back and forth from room to room as the messenger and facilitator.
j. The goal of mediation is to arrive at an agreement between the parties. The agreement will be in writing for all parties to review. Upon agreement, the parties and mediator will sign the agreement which is binding between the parties. Each party and the court will get a copy.
k. The mediation will be terminated by the execution of the agreement, a declaration by the mediator that

further efforts will not be beneficial, or the party or parties to the action declare the mediation is ended.

l. All parties must participate in good faith. No one is asked to commit to settle the case in advance of mediation, but all parties commit to participate in good faith with the intention and goal to resolve the matter.

m. All parties necessary to sign the agreement must be present.

The following case study of mediation titled *Changing Final Divorce Decree* is included to display the power of effective communication when present in a relationship:

> A petition to modify a parent-child relationship was brought by the father and petitioner. The child is the son of the petitioner who had proper standing to this suit. It was believed by the petitioner the modification would be in the child's best interest. The respondent is the child's mother. The order to be modified was entitled Final Decree of Divorce and was rendered on June 30, 2015.
>
> There had been no change of consequence in the status of the child's property since the prior order was rendered. The schooling order to modify was based on a mediated settlement agreement. The child's circumstances affected by the order to be modified materially and substantially changed since the date of the signing of the mediated settlement agreement on which the order to be modified was based.

The Final Decree of Divorce stipulated the child would attend First Baptist School until completion of the fifth grade. The child had been diagnosed with attention deficit hyperactivity disorder. The First Baptist School was incapable by training and specialization of providing the attention and schooling desperately needed in order for the child to fully develop as the school year progressed. The child's situation at First Baptist School became progressively worse. The child was bullied by other students, mocked by other students, and denied recess as an outlet for those physical needs because the school could not protect him from his abusers. By the end of the school year, the child was an emotional wreck.

A child adolescent and adult psychiatrist stated, "It is my professional opinion the child would be emotionally jeopardized by returning to his school of this past year." The petitioner requested the respondent agree to modify the schooling order contained in the Final Decree of Divorce in order that the child could be home schooled collaboratively per the psychiatrist's recommendation. The respondent refused and continued to refuse to consider any modification to the schooling order.

This case was complicated and had been to the judge on numerous occasions without agreement. The judge assigned the case to mediation. By following the rules and guidelines of mediation as noted above, the petitioner and the responder agreed the best interest of the child was to be homeschooled on a collaborative basis for one year.

An adult-to-adult mature conversation requires critical agreements, which are sometimes called ground rules. In the game of baseball, ground rules are special rules particular to each baseball park where the game is played. The playing area extends to the outfield fence in fair playing territory and to out-of-bounds territory where there is seating for fans. The unique design of each ball park requires that rules be defined for situations when areas or objects may interfere with the ball in play or with the participants. There are rights and responsibilities for all involved parties in baseball and also in an adult-to-adult conversation.

The ability to communicate effectively with others is essential no matter your vocation or relationship status. It has been said that 70 percent of your success is based upon your ability to communicate. Obtain and develop effective communication skills, and you will always stand above the crowd. Mutual communication leads to understanding, personal intimacy, and increased value of others. You will impress your boss, clients, and team. These are the top eight communication skills desired by successful employers for new employees:

1. Be an active, good listener. Pay attention to the words of the other person, ask questions for clarification, and restate the information to understand.
2. Body language, eye contact, hand gestures, and voice inflection convey your message. Demonstrate you are focused on the other person. Be interested, not just interesting.
3. Be clear and concise. State a message in as few words as possible and do not ramble.
4. Smile and be a friend. Be nice, cordial, and polite.
5. Be confidently assertive, but not aggressive.
6. Be empathetic. You may disagree with or not like the other person, but it is important for you to understand

and respect their point of view. You have an obligation to listen to their opinion, as their opinion is important and it matters.

7. Be open-minded and willing to enter a conversation with people you do not agree with.
8. Be able to give and receive feedback and criticism.

At Greystone Preparatory School at Schreiner University, where I teach effective communication, each class creates an honor code and standards of conduct to live by during their year at Greystone. Greystone is a unique program combining focused, intense service and academy preparation with a challenging university education for high school graduates committed to earning their appointment to one of the five federal service academies. Each service academy requires a commitment to a strict honor and conduct code. Benjamin Franklin, at age twenty, created a similar plan and practical guide to live by with his thirteen virtues. Franklin's original list contained twelve virtues, but the list was amended to include humility after he was challenged by a Quaker friend while discussing pride. The list was as follows and included a short definition of the virtue:

1. Temperance. Eat not to dullness; drink not to elevation.
2. Silence. Speak not but what may benefit others or yourself; avoid trifling conversation.
3. Order. Let all your things have their places; let each part of your business have its time.
4. Resolution. Resolve to perform what you ought; perform without fail what you resolve.

5. Frugality. Make no expense but to do good to others or yourself; waste nothing.
6. Industry. Lose no time; be always employed in something useful; cut off all unnecessary actions.
7. Sincerity. Use no hurtful deceit; think innocently and justly, and, if you speak, speak accordingly.
8. Justice. Wrong none by doing injuries or omitting the benefits that are your duty.
9. Moderation. Avoid extremes; forbear resenting injuries so much as you think they deserve.
10. Cleanliness. Tolerate no uncleanliness in body, clothes, or habitation.
11. Tranquility. Be not disturbed at trifles, or at accidents common or unavoidable.
12. Chastity. Rarely use venery but for health or offspring, never to dullness, weakness, or the injury of your own or another's peace or reputation.
13. Humility. Imitate Jesus and Socrates.

Of the thirteen virtues listed above, virtue nine, moderation, is a powerful order. Avoid extremes. Forbear resenting injuries so much as you think they deserve. There are three complex words in the middle of the mandate. Franklin is telling us, "forbear resenting injury" and do not be offended by the actions of others. We are living in our most troubling, extreme time for our nation. We cannot recall any other period when people were so divided and easily offended by other people's perspectives. We must take Franklin's lessons to heart and learn to get along with each other.

There are two key items from Franklin. We need to live life in the middle and avoid extremes. This appears to be a dying art. On a continuum, we are polarized with a concentration of opposing extremes of interest. The idea of living in the middle with some sense of compromise is appalling to many people. They are horrified to even think about it. They find their identity in extremes, which can be very dangerous. The second key item is to abstain, overlook, or refrain from the extreme viewpoints of other people and forbear resenting injuries. We must moderate our desire to be offended by letting offensive ideas leave our mind as quickly as we can.

The small things turn into big things. There is no middle ground in the culture of extremes. There is love or hate. There is no occasion which justifies hate. There is integrity or hypocrisy. There is no injustice which warrants bitterness and sorrow. We need to measure our reactions. Are we offended by the statements or viewpoints of the opposition? Moderation is harder than we think or imagine it should be. We must take time to ponder, think, and respond. It takes a very strong person to stand firmly in the middle.

Living in early twentieth-first century America, a large part of the population complains about many things and lives with anger, aggression, and bitterness, which could lead to global violence. Anger motivates and energizes us to action. Broadcast commentators are threatening and volatile. With a slight provocation, anger explodes into a physical attack. The planet is full of hostility. This global problem starts in the local neighborhoods. It is in the schools, churches, movie theaters, and workplaces, and on highways and jogging trails. Lots of places once believed to be safe and secure are now full of harm and risk.

Anger is everywhere—in politics, the media, schools, homes, and churches. The tremendous rise in anger should be a concern to all of us. Anger is not healthy and is not right. In James 1:19–20, from the Living Bible, "Dear brothers, don't ever forget that it is best to listen much, speak little, and not become angry; for anger doesn't make us good, as God demands that we must be." The proper growing conditions to increase our faith and to grow in the Lord occur when we are quick to hear, slow to speak, and slow to anger. Anger does not lead to right living. Anger creates negativity. When we are angry, we stop listening and growing, say negative words, hurt people, and damage ourselves.

In 2 Timothy, Chapter 3, Paul wrote to Timothy:

> "… in the last days it is going to be very difficult ... For people will love only themselves and their money; they will be proud and boastful, sneering at God, disobedient to their parents, ungrateful to them, and thoroughly bad. They will be hardheaded and never give in to others; they will be constant liars and troublemakers and will think nothing of immorality. They will be rough and cruel, and sneer at those who try to be good. They will betray their friends; they will be hotheaded, puffed up with pride …"

Each day, under the world's system for life, there is an exchange for our troubles and concerns. The world system only brings temporary relief. The world system approach makes trouble and is masked by drugs, excessive alcohol, horoscopes, and mindless entertainment. The world's culture believes if you disagree with the lifestyle of others, you must hate or fear them. Additionally, to love someone means you agree with everything they believe or do.

The world's plan is not personal and not designed with you in mind. People you do not know and who are supposedly smarter than you, originated it. A select few designed, created, and showcased what is and is not in the plan. You were not invited. If you are invited, there will be no outside ideas recognized or heard. There is no optimism in the worldly plan. Divorce, debt, crime, terrorism, and sickness are rampant. People are looking for hope in all the wrong places. "Houston, we have a problem."

There is no middle ground in politics, religion, or relationships. The middle class and common sense appear to be dying. Common sense is not common practice. There are religious zealots versus atheists. Our culture is full of extremism. We have superlatives to describe everything from sports to politics to weather. Many dangers lurk in this hideous trend.

With all these negative events and attitudes, there is still hope. We are highly educated, but we have difficulty communicating our thoughts and hearing what others mean and are communicating to us. We need to assess our communicating skills and review our thought patterns. "We are what we think," said American Radio Speaker and Author Earl Nightingale.

Fear and doubt may cause you to share very few conversations. I believe effective communication is a highly emotional contact sport and a teachable skill. If you feel comfortable and confident, you can easily communicate your thoughts, values, and beliefs. It is my belief that we can solve a lot of problems if we obtain gumption and learn to communicate on a high-road level with adult-to-adult, one-to-one, face-to-face conversations. Effective communication builds strong relationships, and strong relationships must be built on a solid foundation of trust.

THE COMMON THREAD

INTEGRITY

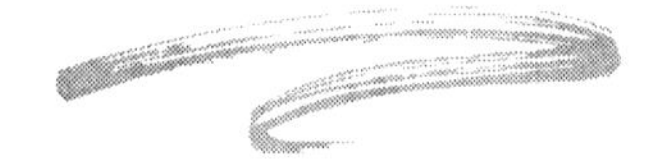

"Integrity is choosing your thoughts and actions based on values rather than personal gain."

—Chris Karcher, American author and speaker

Integrity is number one in all things. Everything else is number two. *Webster's Dictionary* defines integrity as the quality of being honest and fair; the state of being complete, whole, and undivided. The moral definition of integrity is doing the right thing, at the right time, even when no one is looking.

Let's look at the word "integrity" from a spiritual perspective. The Hebrew words, "*Shalom*" or "*Shalem*," refer to everything being as it should be. In the case of individual integrity, it means that each person is upright and truthful, dependable, honest, and just. They display the moral and spiritual qualities of wisdom and maturity. It also means each person has wholeness and is united within themselves; there is no internal conflict.

Synonyms for "*shalom*" and "*shalem*" are "*Tam*" and "*tamim*," Hebrew words for "blameless," often translated as sincere, perfect, blemish-free, and of integrity. The Hebrew word "*Tam*" is repeated in the Hebrew Bible multiple times. It is in the book of Job seven times, as Job is described as a good, upright, and blameless man. There are many people described with integrity in the Bible. Integrity denotes wholeness. A person with integrity has it all together in one unified piece. They are consistent and congruent. They are the same yesterday, today, and tomorrow. They use the same value system for all questions, concerns, and choices in life.

Healthy relationships are built on integrity, maintaining a positive attitude, eliminating pointing the finger with criticism and condemnation, accepting responsibility, and by applying the "golden rule" of treating others the way you want to be treated, or, as the Bible (or Jesus) put it, "Do to others what you would have them do to you" (Matthew 7:12 NIV).

Integrity requires us to discover who we are, claim who we are, and live who we are without pretending to be another person, and the structural definition speaks of the force the structure can withstand or the strength of something's foundation. In contrast to the meaning of the word integrity is the meaning of the word hypocrisy. While integrity means whole, complete, and congruent, hypocrisy means divided—pretending to be in heart and soul something you are not and acting a part, as if in a play. In our current culture, integrity matters because all that remains without integrity is hypocrisy. As we can see clearly from the definition provided here, with hypocrisy, bad things happen.

Let's take a look at some of the consequences of a life without integrity, the consequences of hypocrisy.

ENRON CORPORATION

In 1985, Enron Corporation was founded by Kenneth L. Lay out of a merger between Lay's Houston Natural Gas and InterNorth, both of which were relatively small, regional companies in the Texas area. Enron was a symbol of civic pride in both local Houston and the world financial markets, and Lay was known to have close ties to the Bush family. But his aspirations of power did not stop there. Lay wanted to be the most successful executive in the United States with the most important company in the world, and, seemingly, Lay accomplished what he set out to do. Together with Jeffery Skilling (who was Enron's president/COO and succeeded Lay as CEO), Lay built a company that appeared to have everything—money, power, new ideas, and a leadership team with aligned goals of power and grandeur.

Enron's motto was "Respect, Integrity, Communication and Excellence." Its vision and values mission statement declared, "We treat others as we would like to be treated ourselves.... We do not tolerate abusive or disrespectful treatment. Ruthlessness, callousness and arrogance don't belong here." For six consecutive years, from 1996 to 2001, *Fortune* magazine named Enron the most innovative company in America. As one might expect, based on his corporation's motto, Lay was even on the cover of *Continental Airlines* magazine as a person of integrity.

The public loved Enron and placed Lay and Skilling in high regard as top-notch leaders in community and business. Then, on May 25, 2006, Lay and Skilling were found guilty of fraud, bank fraud, insider trading, and conspiracy emerging from a number of other company scandals involving get-rich-quick schemes and management malfeasance during the 1990s. Each conviction carried a sentence of up to ten years in prison.

So, what went wrong? In early 2000, the top level of Enron management lied, misrepresented financial and economic information, and cheated many people out of millions of dollars of savings and retirement income dollars. Most of Enron's 29,000 employees lost all of their retirement funds from 401Ks invested in Enron stock. Beyond that, the company once considered "the darling of Wall Street" fell out of favor with the trading giant. The people who had viewed Enron and its leaders in such a high regard felt betrayed. Enron's motto of "Respect, Integrity, Communication and Excellence" became a statement viewed by the public as hypocrisy, and Kenneth Lay and Skilling were viewed as hypocrites.

A lack of integrity in personal relationships creates mistrust, anger, and non-existent communication. Distrust is suspicion of character, agenda, capabilities, and track record.

To grasp the full context of integrity, it is also important to understand the distinction between responding and reacting, and the role each plays in either contributing to integrity or tearing it down.

Responding builds strong relationships because we measure, think, and select our words thoughtfully and act in ways that build positive relationships. Relationships grow stronger where there is trust and encouragement.

Reacting, on the other hand, creates an environment of fear, negativity, and mistrust through thoughtless actions and words. In reacting, we use our instincts, and all the trouble in the relationship become the other person's fault. People act like victims and do not take responsibility for their actions. Relationships erode in the "blame game" environment. Abraham Lincoln, the sixteenth president of the United States of America, said it best, "You cannot escape the responsibility of tomorrow by evading it today."

Integrity is formed when all your aspirations, all your wants are focused in one direction. A life of integrity is not easy, but a life of integrity is simple. Do the right thing—figure it out and do it.

American folk hero Davy Crockett said, "First be sure you're right, then go ahead." Integrity is number one, all other considerations are second. Integrity is displayed when we say what we mean and mean what we say. (In Texas, we say, "walk your talk.") It is all about taking personal responsibility for individual actions and being a positive example for others. Living a life of integrity brings many benefits such as joy, contentment, and satisfaction with nothing to hide or fear. You will become known as loyal and someone who can be counted on in times of need.

You must be the right person, do the right things, and then, and only then, can you have all this world has to offer. Integrity means being whole, unbroken, and undivided. All parts of the personality come together so there is no split in the inner being. A divided soul occurs when part of you wants to do one thing while the other parts of you want to do something else.

TRUST

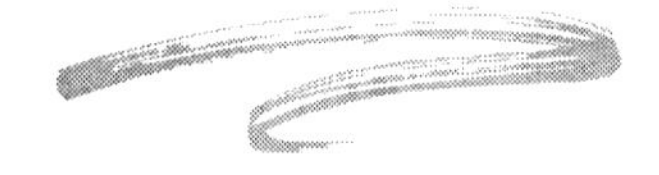

"Trust is confidence in the integrity and abilities of others."

—Kenneth O'Neal

Trust does not exist without integrity, and integrity does not exist without trust. All great relationships have trust as the foundation. The four most common elements of relationships required to initiate trust are:

- qualified ability and knowledge
- honest dependability
- adherence to moral and ethical principles with high character

- an interchange of thoughts and opinions by speech and writing.

In order to establish trust, a leader must issue guidelines to create an environment for dialogue and continued, transparent conversation. There should be no criticism, prejudgment, or jumping to conclusions.

As stated earlier, the number one problem in the world is people not being willing to take responsibility for their actions. The "blame game" goes back to the beginning of time as recorded in the Bible's book of Genesis.

When God placed Adam and Eve in the Garden of Eden, He told them they could have it all, except they were not to eat the fruit of the Tree of Knowledge in the middle of the garden. However, they ate the tree's fruit, and in the evening, as God walked in the garden, He called for Adam, and Adam responded, "Over here, Lord."

Then God asked the question, "Adam, did you eat the fruit of the tree in the middle of the garden?" God already knew the answer, but He wanted Adam to respond.

Adam, however, did the "manly thing" and replied, "Lord, let me tell you about that woman you gave me," and that is where the ball started its long, unending roll. God then asked Eve if she had eaten the fruit, and Eve passed it along saying, "Let me tell you about that snake," and of course, when He asked, the snake did not have a leg to stand on. I know I am in error from a theological stance when I make that statement. However, I am not in error when I say that each one of us must recognize that it is not, "his fault, her fault, or their fault." It is our responsibility.

The "golden rule" is to do unto others as you would have them do unto you. In other words, treat others like you want to be treated. We all want to be treated with kindness, respect, courtesy, love, and appreciation. Build your relationships based on the philosophy of doing and serving others and also looking for the good in others. Look for the positive characteristics in all people. The more we look for the good qualities, the more good qualities we will find. Always praise the performer publicly and criticize the bad performance privately.

One of the most important aspects of all relationships is trust. It is the number one characteristic people want in a partner, spouse, or significant other. Trust makes human connections perform at a high level of excellence. Trust is built with bonding and developing a rapport. Rapport is the process of having sincere interest in others, listening at a synergistic level, and reflecting and nurturing to develop a rapid and lasting bond for the relationship's duration.

Strong feelings of trust are built in small portions when we choose our important relationships over other interactions. Trust is important because it requires us to be vulnerable. The small, two-letter word, "we," is significant in creating trust. Be personal. To establish trust, a conversation should not be one-sided. Be plainspoken. It is your fault if they do not understand. Be positive. Build their self-esteem. Be honest and candid. No one in this life is perfect. We have all sinned and frequently fall short of God's will.

Integrity is the number one characteristic of a person of gumption. The byproduct of integrity is trust. You can rely on a person with gumption. A person of gumption follows the essentials of a fulfilling, meaningful, joyful, and rich, winning relationship. They are loving and committed to a well-balanced and meaningful life. They have a serving attitude and a good heart for all people. They are open and honest, approaching people with friendship and cheer. A gumptious person is patient, enduring, sustaining, and persevering, with vibrant hope there is victory in the end. The possibilities that emerge from life's circumstances provide the endurance to carry on to the finish line. Gumptious people are close in their relationships and lead with integrity and empathy. Gumption is not just an attitude or a good feeling, gumption is an intentional lifestyle of fairness and goodness.

All great relationships have trust as the foundation. The four most common elements of collaborative relationships required to initiate trust are competence, reliability, integrity, and communication. These four items are needed to create a sustainable and successful relationship.

ATTITUDE OF GRATITUDE

"The only disability in life is a bad attitude."

—Scott Hamilton

ATTITUDE

The primary force determining if you succeed or fail as a person of gumption is your attitude, as you have complete control over it. Your response to what happens to you and who you become is more important than the event.

American businessman W. Clement Stone wrote, "There is little difference in people, but that little difference makes a big difference. The little difference is attitude. The big difference is whether it is positive or negative."

A positive mental attitude is a most outstanding asset. While I believe time is your most valuable asset, a positive mental attitude is another outstanding one. For this discussion, let's define attitude as a habit of an individual act of thinking. Self-talk is the way we talk to ourselves. My friend Dr. Shad Helmstetter wrote a powerful book, *What To Say When You Talk To Yourself,* demonstrating new techniques to program your potential for total success. Impacted by self-talk, your mindset forms your attitude, and your attitude affects everything you do.

Making choices is a part of life. You have to decide to make changes. Changes in the way you think will change your attitude. By changing your attitude, you will change your behavior and actions. Change in actions will change your results, and when your attitude improves or gets better, so do your circumstances.

Believe in yourself with an 'I CAN' approach.
Never quit and success will come.

I have learned that attitude is everything. One of the most valuable assets you have is a positive mental attitude. Your attitude today determines your success.

Your attitude produces behavior. What you do is directly related to what you become as a person and what you accomplish in life. An important key to success is to treat everybody like you want to be treated.

Attitudes are contagious. You must protect your attitude by being around positive people who support you, read the right books, and listen to the right music. My grandmother always told me, "Birds of a feather flock together." Be careful when selecting your associates.

"BELIEVE IN YOURSELF WITH AN 'I CAN' APPROACH. NEVER QUIT AND SUCCESS WILL COME."

DEVELOP A HABIT OF GRATITUDE

"Express your gratitude and never forget.
Do not just speak words. Live by them."

—John F. Kennedy

Gratitude is defined as a feeling of appreciation or thankfulness and is described by Zig Ziglar as "the healthiest of all human emotions." I have been on a journey of gratitude for a long time. The more you express gratitude for what you have, the more likely you will receive even more about which to be grateful.

CEO of Ziglar, Inc., Tom Ziglar says, "The quickest way to success is to replace bad habits with good habits." We need to make gratitude a habit, but people often tend to resist change, so forming healthy habits takes time and dedication.

According to a 2009 study published in *The European Journal of Social Psychology*, it takes eighteen to two hundred and fifty-four days to create a habit. On average, it takes about sixty-six days for a new behavior to become automatic. Each day I write down three things I am grateful for on a list in my daily journal. Each day the three things are different from the ones listed before. If you make a list like this for sixty-six days, you will have almost 200 items you are grateful for, and your mind will constantly be looking for new things for which to be grateful and thankful.

Some days, when I am thinking, preparing, and planning, I enjoy reflecting on the things I have been thankful for in the past. Here is an example of the way that time spent reflecting turns to gratitude:

"EXPRESS YOUR GRATITUDE AND NEVER FORGET. DO NOT JUST SPEAK WORDS. LIVE BY THEM."

- JOHN F. KENNEDY

Those who know me well, know my love of Southern Gospel Quartet Music. My favorite has always been Hovie Lister and the Statesmen. When I was able, I would attend practice sessions with the Statesmen and Blackwood Brothers at The Briarcliff Hotel. I especially enjoyed their bass singer, James "Big Chief" Wetherington. He was dignified and a class act with integrity; his character was beyond reproach. "Big Chief" was a wonderful man, from a little South Georgia town called Ty, who enjoyed the outdoors, hunting, and fishing. On many occasions we would spend entire days together at Fulton County Stadium watching the Atlanta Braves. "Big Chief" had many followers, and they all seemed to love baseball, too. Many life lessons are learned on the field and in the stands. I am grateful Abner Doubleday invented baseball.

"Big Chief" believed he was called by God to sing and to use his voice to inspire and bless others. I will never forget our conversations. He believed, "Life is like a mountain railroad from cradle to grave." He prayed "for all to understand that the Hope of America lies in faith in God and The Common Man." I learned many soul lessons from "Big Chief," and I am grateful for our friendship.

LIVING A WELL-BALANCED LIFE

Consider all aspects of your life: mental input, character development, physical ability, family relationships, personal energy, career, and financial.

For several years, each Monday I could be heard on the local KERV radio station in Kerrville, Texas, broadcasting "Living a Well-Balanced Life." The opening session started with Louis Armstrong singing "What a Wonderful World" and included a statement of gratitude, noting at least three items in my daily journal. I have many things for which to be thankful. Some of my favorites are listed below:

1. "America the Beautiful," the land of the free and the home of the brave. A land of people from all walks of life. Each person shares the common bond of living in a free enterprise system, enabling them to more fully use their God-given abilities.
2. The plan of salvation.
3. My family, especially my four grown children, all college graduates and employed at worthwhile work.

People are creatures of habit and tend to act in the same manner in similar situations. I urge anyone resistant to change to remember the words of American business magnate Henry Ford when he said, "If you always do what you've always done, you'll always get what you've always got." To be better, we must do better in order to give to others and create a legacy to last through eternity. Becoming a person of gumption doesn't happen without a willingness to change.

"IT TAKES A STRONG, COURAGEOUS PERSON TO FORGIVE; THE GREATEST GIFT TO YOURSELF IS FORGIVENESS."

- KENNETH O'NEAL

FORGIVENESS

"It takes a strong, courageous person to forgive;
The greatest gift to yourself is forgiveness."

—Kenneth O'Neal

Forgiveness is the act of pardoning an offender and letting go of resentment. It is giving up any claim to be compensated for the hurt or loss suffered in the offense. Forgiveness is a choice. Absorbing the hurt and pain is paying the debt and extending grace to someone who deserves revenge and punishment. Forgiveness is an opening to peace of mind. Finding the door of forgiveness is an arduous task.

How do we deal with the anger, resentment, and pain of betrayal, injury, or rejection from someone we love?

After the divorce filing by my ex-wife, I had a broken heart, shattered dreams, desires for revenge, guilt, and shame. It was the worst experience of my life. When someone commits an infraction against us, we often have a tendency to take the mindset that the person is now our debtor. We tend to think they owe us an apology, compensation, and restoration of lost items. I was wounded, and my ex-wife's memory lived deep in the crevices of my inner being. Receiving forgiveness is a wonderful feeling, but extending forgiveness is different. I reacted to the divorce, the loss, and the adversity by falling to pieces, bemoaning my fate, and seething at my ex-wife. With no one to turn to, I was distraught. I then went to God as my only hope. He encouraged and strengthened me.

We want the one who hurt us to be punished and pay the debt we think they owe to us. When someone harms us, especially emotionally, we face a dilemma. A part of us wants to get even—to pay the person back, to get revenge, and to lower ourselves to their level. We feel justified in getting back at someone who has harmed us. We feel morally compromised. People are drawn to revenge. It is a natural instinct we do not have to choose. Revenge is natural, but creates undesirable health.

Unforgiveness will turn you into someone you never intended to be. You will become a different person, displaying attitudes and characteristics detected in harmful and evil people.

It is only natural and easy to dismiss the statement, "I will forgive, but I will never forget." This is a major problem, though, as this common reaction for many creates real tragedy. It is not a supernatural response.

Many people today, especially married couples, coexist for years in abrasive silence. They stop speaking to each other. This is a major result of refusing to forgive and forget. Denial and saying no to reconciliation build remembrance of contempt and hatred. We disclose our servant heart to the offending party based on reaction or response. Reaction is instinctive, thoughtless, and lives in an environment of fear. Response, though, is a posture of wholeness and lives in an environment of strong relationships.

Forgive and forget is mentioned in the Bible many times. See Hebrew 8:12 (KJV), which says, "For I will be merciful to their unrighteousness, and their sins and their iniquities will I remember no more". God invites us to leave our burdens at the cross. In Isaiah 43:25 (NIV), He assures us that He, "blots out your transgressions, for my own sake, and remembers your sins no more." Another verse is Jeremiah 31:34, "… I will forgive their wickedness and will remember their sins no more." I am not sure forgetting is humanly possible, as we have many natural limitations, but we can forgive.

A closer look will disclose the use of the word servant representing a person of the supernatural, living God. The worldly plan is ruled by Satan who keeps telling us lies full of hatred and bitterness. Satan directs us back to pain and suffering. I mentor and coach many members of reconnect programs for alcohol and drug abuse. Yes, we recognize the problem and name it. Then we do the best we can to forget the abuse, ugliness, pain, and suffering of each situation. These are events, and they do not identify who we are and who we can become through the power of a supernatural God. Through submission and surrender, people's lives are under His control. God knows the situations and has a plan.

English theologian and evangelist John Wesley said in his writings that we should continue to work toward perfection. I fail and fall short, but it does not keep me from trying.

To become whole, you must forgive yourself first. Release the need to replay a negative situation over and over in your mind. Do not become a hostage to your past by always reviewing and reliving your mistakes. Do not remind yourself of what should have, could have, or would have been. Release those thoughts and let them go. Move on.

A RELIABLE INNER COMPASS

"Knowing and understanding your purpose is a true compass."

—Kenneth O'Neal

CHARACTER

Character makes up the moral and mental qualities distinctive to an individual. Honesty, responsibility, and courage are admirable qualities possessed by someone with character. The six pillars of character are: trustworthiness, respect, responsibility, fairness, caring, and citizenship. Life is a moral and spiritual journey, and we have a reliable inner compass known as the soul, a directional compass for life.

LEGACY

The Choose to Win Mentorship Program at The Greystone Academy Preparatory School at Schreiner Institute was established to transform the lives of cadet candidates, one choice at a time. The program was based on the philosophy and writings of one of the greatest motivators, teachers, and success mentors in history, Zig Ziglar. His message of encouragement and lifelong investment in helping others made a positive impact on millions of lives around the world.

As Ziglar Legacy Certified coaches, trainers, and mentors for the Choose to Win Program, we begin with the desires, ambitions, and why a young person would want to serve as an officer in the United States military. We believe the cadet must understand life as a journey that starts with survival and expands across stability, success, and significance, ending with the creation of legacy. Mark Batterson said it best: "Inheritance is what you leave to someone. Legacy is what you leave in someone."

Achieving their appointment to an academy or a commission from ROTC requires the right mindset, strategy, and actions. We believe the cadets can achieve a well-balanced, successful life and leave a legacy to survive through eternity.

I believe, along with Zig Ziglar, his son, Tom, and the millions of people who follow Ziglar's philosophies, that you can apply these teachings to your life work and your personal life to achieve success. This is paramount in earning a commission through ROTC or an appointment to one of the five military service academies. I am a United States Air Force veteran, having served as a noncommissioned officer at Langley Air Force

Base with the 316th Tactical Airlift Wing, conducting airplane replacement training and becoming an operational tactical airlift wing with three squadrons of C-130 Hercules aircraft. Additionally, I served in Vietnam with Headquarters 7th Air Force at Tan Son Nhut AB, SVN in communications. Serving our great nation is all about God, honor, and duty.

My father was a United States Marine who served during World War II, although he was the strong, silent type and said very little about his military service. There were many black and white pictures depicting scenes in the battlefield that were never discussed or explained. I understood he was in charge of the motor pool. He told me of attending a small school in south central Georgia where he remembered a plaque on the wall with these words:

Be careful of your thoughts, for your thoughts become your words.
Be careful of your words, for your words become your deeds.
Be careful of your deeds, for your deeds become your habits.
Be careful of your habits, for your habits become your character.
Be careful of your character, for your character becomes your destiny.

Destiny, legend, and legacy are sometimes used as synonyms, but they are very different. Destiny is a predetermined state or condition foreordained by the divine creator or by human will.

A legend is left by what you do and is established by the things you do, the things you create, and what you are known for doing in your life. A legacy is who you really are and the things you leave in others through experiences and foundational belief systems.

In his famous "I Have a Dream" speech, civil rights activist and minister Martin Luther King, Jr. spoke of that day to come when all Americans "will not be judged by the color of their skin, but by the content of their character." I think Dr. King's reference to character speaks to the virtues of wisdom, justice, fortitude, self-control, love, positivity, strong work ethic, integrity, gratitude, and humility. These are all virtues held dear by the person of gumption.

THE JOURNEY TO GUMPTION

THE "WORK IN PROGRESS" LIFE

"The greatest glory in living lies not in never falling, but in rising every time we fall."

—Nelson Mandela

A maternal grandmother full of the Holy Spirit, a mother with six children, and a father who served in the United States Marine Corps and who took his family to church three times a week were the figureheads in my childhood. It was a hot, humid Sunday night in June in south central Georgia when the traveling Pentecostal evangelist gave an altar call. At age thirteen,

I walked the church aisle and publically surrendered my heart to God. At the time, I thought I was a good person. However, I did not understand the decision I made, and no one at the church instructed me on the God who sent His son to Earth to pay the price with His life for my sins so I could have eternal life. The scenario was foreign to me.

Due to my father's work in the Marine Corps, our family moved to central Florida where I finished high school and one year of college. There were two significant happenings in my life after my conversion as a young teenager. The first was when my younger sister died from pneumonia and infantile paralysis. The second happening occurred in my senior year of high school, when I was involved in a major car accident. I considered myself a good Christian. I was considerate, kind, respectful, honored my mother and father, and tried hard to always do the right thing. I recall questioning, "Why did bad things happen to me?" and "Where was God?"

At this time, I began to think about my life and God's intent and purpose for me. I was involved in church, associated with the right people, and never smoked or consumed alcohol. Still, I knew I was not close to God. I was uncertain, indecisive, and could not totally connect with God. I struggled and was disobedient. I was prideful and did not know what to do with God.

I completed four years in the United States Air Force and earned a business administration degree in accounting. I became a certified public accountant in Atlanta, Georgia. During this time, I continued to attend church and read my Bible. I still did not feel whole. I knew something was missing. I was searching. Why was God not working on my behalf? Where was God?

I advised many business owners on taking their company public and selling stock shares on the exchange. I left public accounting to start a business coaching and consulting firm. I bought businesses, sold businesses, and worked with business owners in their businesses. Many opportunities came to me. I doubted God and never asked Him to help. I believed I knew what and how to do everything. There was some success, but it never seemed to be the "home run." There were some large failures. I lost a significant construction company due to bad management and the economic downturn in the real estate market, and I lost my family. My wife filed for divorce.

I was devastated. Where was God? I thought I was a good man as I went to church and read my Bible. I was nice and tried to help people. Then one day, the pain of hopelessness and helplessness became too much. I sought God and cried out for deliverance. I admitted my wrongdoings. I confessed my unbelief and self-reliance. I meditated on God and made a commitment to follow His ways. I prayed, I wept, and I read the Bible, searching to hear from God. American Minister and Author Raymond Edman wrote about J. Hudson Taylor's *The Exchanged Life*:

> "The deep dealing of God with His children varies in detail, but the general pattern seems much alike for individual cases. Into each life there arises an awareness of failure, a falling short of all that one should be in the Lord: then there is a definite meeting with the risen Savior in utter surrender of heart, which is indeed death to self."

At this point, I trusted God. I now knew one day the helpless feeling would go away and I would be full of joy and contentment. I now knew I was not a good man.

I spent the majority of my business career working in accounting for two certified public accounting firms while living in Atlanta, Georgia, and Houston, Texas, where I founded my own firm and worked primarily with small public companies across the United States. In addition to the accounting practice, I presented around twenty seminars and workshops each year on various business topics from auditing, taxes, financial statements, and forms required by the Securities and Exchange Commission. I thoroughly enjoyed the work, especially the personal interaction with clients and the accounting staff. In the eyes of my peers and the outside world, I appeared to be successful and happy. However, I did not realize the real opportunity for success resided within me.

I had all the characteristics necessary for success, but I did not recognize the traits, so I could not claim them. Finally, though, I realized success was within me the whole time. It could not come from the job or the accounting firm. Success, joy, and happiness are not matters of chance, but matters of choice.

During the majority of my business career, I noticed that no matter how successful I became, I never found the same success at home. I spent most of my adult working life frustrated with my inability to succeed and win at home. I was a winner at work and considered an expert in taking small companies public through original public offerings or reverse mergers. On one occasion, staff of the firm and I filed fifty original filings to go public. My frustration and inability to thrive at home led me to travel more and more and to work longer periods out of town.

While in town, I worked long hours and weekends. The joke at work was, "I was the person in charge of the accounting practice, but I was not the head of my family." It was easier to be the chief executive at work than to be the chief executive at home.

The accounting practice was the business world of generally acceptable accounting principles, tax regulation, and business strategies related to mergers and acquisitions. The family and home environment was a world of chaos, drama, arguments, disappointments, and disagreements. At one point in my disjointed success, the accounting firm represented thirty-eight small- to medium-sized public companies geographically spread over the United States from Boston, Massachusetts, to Newport Beach, California. I personally managed these accounts for the firm.

In the early 1990s, I was notified by the Securities and Exchange Commission that one of the clients was under investigation for fraudulent financial statements and illegal acts. The work papers related to their audits were subpoenaed, and it was determined the audit staff had failed to visit and examine a wholly owned subsidiary. The net assets of the subsidiary were overstated by the parent company.

I was the owner and founder of the firm and responsible for my staff's actions. I agreed to testify for the United States government against my former client. The president of the company was convicted on more than one hundred securities violations and released on bail to settle his personal affairs before going to prison. The judge requested my opinion on setting bail for him, and I told the judge it would be a mistake. Bail was given against my wishes, and the president of the public company was found dead in a Mexico City hotel within the next month.

Time and Money Management

"Time is more valuable than money. You can get more money, but you cannot get more time."

—Jim Rohn, American Entrepreneur

How many times have you heard from a friend, "I have no time and I have no money"? These are the two excuses used by people when invited to go somewhere or do something by a friend. Let's look at time.

TIME MANAGEMENT

Time is your most important asset. Time management is a mi[illegible] nomer. We cannot manage time, we cannot store time. Time management is life management. We all have twenty-four hours each day. The majority of our time is spent sleeping (six to eight hours), working (eight to ten hours), and watching television (four to five hours). Most successful people agree time is their most valuable asset. Once time is gone, it is gone forever. You cannot earn more time. Self-discipline is required to become skilled in managing life. The answer to time management is prioritizing the use of your time by performing top priority items.

The learned skill of managing your time will determine your success or failure as an officer in the armed services, a president of a major corporation, or a leader in your family. Time is required in everything you have to do. Time cannot be saved and cannot be recovered once it is lost. The better you use your time, the more you will achieve in all you do. Your rewards will be great. Most of us undervalue the time we have been given.

The management of your time is essential for professional and personal effectiveness. Your level of peace, harmony, and mental well-being will be greater when you are in control of your time. An "out of control" feeling is the major source of stress, anxiety, and depression in our daily lives. The better you are at controlling the day-to-day events, the better you will feel, the more energy you will have, the better you will sleep, and more projects will be completed.

Time management skills are learned. The ideas and methods I teach, if used properly, will help you gain many productive hours and double your output and productivity. Your work is important. It is imperative you establish significant blocks of time for major projects and specific tasks. Here are suggestions to improve effectiveness and efficiency by creating blocks of time:

- First, work in the morning when you are fresh and alert.
- Second, allow no interruptions. DO NOT DISTURB signs work well when placed on your door.
- Third, gain an extra hour in the morning by starting work early and an extra hour in the afternoon by staying one hour later. These steps are great when there are major projects with short deadlines to complete.

DISCIPLINE

"For a man to conquer himself is the first and noblest of all victories."

—Plato

Effective discipline is the willingness to force yourself to pay the price, to do what you know you should do, whether you feel like it or not. This willingness is critical for success in becoming the best you. Jim Rohn said, "Discipline is the bridge between goals and accomplishment."

To become an outstanding, self-disciplined time mana
you will need the Four D's of Effectiveness:

1. Desire. You must have an intense, burning desire to get your time under control and to achieve maximum effectiveness.
2. Decision. You must make a clear decision to practice good time management techniques until they become a habit.
3. Determination. You must be willing to persist against all temptations until you have become an effective time manager. Your desire will reinforce your determination.
4. Discipline. You must discipline yourself to make time management a lifelong practice. Self-discipline is the major key to a successful and better you. Effective discipline is the willingness to force yourself to pay the price, to do what you know you should do whether you feel like it or not. This willingness is critical for success to become the best you.

Learning time management skills and becoming an excellent time manager is huge. Winners in life use time well. One of the most important rules for success is to form good habits and make them your master. Form good habits and let them form you into the best you.

Remember, time management is really life management. Good time management and personal productivity begin by valuing your life and every minute of it.

You must work hard at managing yourself, as you cannot manage time. Within your twenty-four hours each day, you uld take time to self-evaluate and to identify your top iorities. Those purpose-producing activities should move to the top of your list. Here are some questions you might ask yourself as you prepare to plan and reflect on the important things in life:

- Do you have written goals with action steps to be taken?
- Do you use and set deadlines effectively?
- How do you manage stress and times of boredom?
- Do you start and finish each project strong?

I believe you can do all you want to do on your list of goals. I just do not think you can do them all in one day. If you want to always perform at a high level of excellence in all things, you can only work on four to six items each day. When responding to the pertinent question, "what is important and what is urgent?" I have adapted a form of General Dwight David Eisenhower's Decision Matrix, which divides all activities into four categories:

1. Important and Urgent—pressing problems and crisis situations; most problems settle here after a while as projects driven by deadlines.
2. Important and Not Urgent—preparing to plan; planning the work; building winning relationships; working the plan. Here is where you receive the greatest return on your time usage. This area is positive, proactive, and in a controlled atmosphere. This area is where you should invest your time.
3. Not Important and Urgent—interruptions and some telephone calls; meetings, mail, and reports.

This category must be avoided and can be omitted w correct choices are made. Most of the time spent in th area is because of temporary conditions.

4. Not Important and Not Urgent—reading and watching television; some phone calls and mail; items of procrastination. This area is packed with temporary situations. The best way to handle items here is to say, "No." Eisenhower said items in this area should be filed in the trash can and discarded.

The Decision Matrix helps the user to be responsive instead of reactive to tasks and situations. Items contributing to long-term goals are categorized as "important" and should be completed in the appropriate time frame. In my adaptation of Eisenhower's Decision Matrix, I layer each quadrant with a formula that quantifies the return on the time investment (ROI) on tasks within each category. By maintaining my focus on activities categorized as "important," I am better able to respond instead of react. This allows me to remain calm, positive, and open to new opportunities, resulting in a higher rate of return in these categories.

Tasks requiring immediate attention are categorized as "urgent" and place you in a reaction mode with a defensive, negative, and narrow mindset on future opportunities, thus reducing the return on your time investment. Using my adaptation, let us imagine the amount of time invested in each of the four quadrants above as a monetary value of a hundred dollars. By doing so, you are now able to clear results, which would be as follows: ((final value – initial value)/cost)(100)

1. Important and Urgent: 0% ROI
   a. Investment Amount: $100.00
   b. Return Value: $100.00
2. Important and Not Urgent: 100% ROI
   a. Investment Amount: $100.00
   b. Return Value: $200.00
3. Not important and Urgent: –50%
   a. Investment Amount: $100.00
   b. Return Value: $50.00
4. Not Important and Not Urgent: –100% ROI
   a. Investment Amount: $100.00
   b. Return Value: $0

Based on the above examples, clearly the best principle here is to strive to only work and invest your time on activities and tasks in the "important and not-urgent" category. As long as you have an item unfinished and open to work on, do not move to any other area. By investing your time in the "important and not-urgent" category, you will feel better, be in better health, and accomplish more on a daily basis.

MONEY MANAGEMENT

Have you ever had the thought, "I do not have the money to pay for my gym membership?" If you have, you are not alone, as that is one of the top excuses people provide when asked why they don't go to the gym to improve their health. Attitudes toward money must be changed from scarcity to abundance. Spending money on yourself for improving health and wellness

is not an expense, but an investment in your life. This me
there needs to be a change in perspective regarding money.

There are two prevalent attitudes toward money:

1. Optimism and abundance, which leads to financial success. People with this attitude save, they spend less than they earn, they manage credit, they give, and they plan for emergencies.
2. Pessimism and scarcity, which leads to want and financial instability. People with this negative attitude do not save, tend to spend more than they make, do not manage credit and debt, and do not give to others or plan for emergencies.

"A wise person should have money in their head but not in their heart."

—Jonathan Swift

Many people have the wrong idea about money in believing it is evil. In actuality, the Bible states it is the love of and idolizing of money that is evil. What is your attitude toward money and finances? You must begin to view money and earning money as morally good. In addition, it is also morally good to make wise decisions about your finances.

Rabbi Daniel Lapin is the author of *Thou Shalt Prosper and Business Secrets from the Bible*. When talking about money, he says we are often rewarded with a certificate of appreciation called money. The more problems you solve by serving others, the more certificates of appreciation you will receive.

Lapin says, "God is the happiest with His children when ey are serving and solving the problems of His other children." When you solve a problem for someone, you are not only working for them, but you are also working for God. Talents, skills, and experiences are used to solve the problems of His other children. Money is the certificate of appreciation rewarding you for solving the problems of others. There is a moral responsibility to use your money wisely. You are to provide for yourself and your family, as well as those God calls you to help.

Are you in debt? Are you living paycheck to paycheck where an unexpected expense would create a disaster in your life? Your business or your career exists for one reason and only one reason—it is a vehicle to help you achieve your life goals and dreams.

AFFIRMATION: "I am ridiculously in charge of my dreams. I take ownership of my dreams."

1. You have permission from God to dream big. Conceive a dream and believe.
2. See yourself achieving your dreams.
3. Write your dreams on paper.
4. Prioritize your dreams and turn them into goals.
5. Work hard on dreams daily.

A really bad habit is to have no financial goals. Seventy percent of households live paycheck to paycheck.

"If you aim at nothing, you'll hit it every time."

—Zig Ziglar

"IF YOU AIM AT NOTHING, YOU'LL HIT IT EVERY TIME."

- ZIG ZIGLAR

ecent national survey of 3,000 employee workers discovered at 76 percent of hourly workers are living paycheck to paycheck in some capacity. This problem can be solved by working on dreams, desires, and goals.

You must prepare to work, plan your work, and work your plan.

The Four Keys to Make Your Dreams a Reality:

1. Start before you feel ready.
2. Divide big dreams into small steps.
3. Become comfortable with uncertainty.
4. Change your perspective—create a mental movie of you in the middle of your dream.

"Never spend your money before you have it."

—Thomas Jefferson, *Control of Finances*

You must take control of your finances one small baby step at a time. American personal finance personality Dave Ramsey is one of my favorite people when it comes to money. These seven steps for money management are on his website and documented in his book, *Financial Peace.*

1. Create an emergency fund of $1,000.00.
   This fund is for unexpected events which happen daily in life such as an issue with plumbing at home. If you cannot place $1,000 in a separate fund, start somewhere with as little as $10.00. You can be ready for the unknown.

2. Pay off all debts except for the home mortgage, incl ing credit cards.
   Your plan is to list all of your debts in order, from the lowest balance to the highest. Ramsey suggests starting with the smallest without regard to the interest rates.
3. Set aside six months of expenses in a savings account.
   As part of your budget planning, calculate the amount you need to live without a job or income for six months. This is where you create a full emergency plan. The majority of families need $12,000—$15,000.
4. Invest 15% of your income into a retirement account.
   At this time, with a full emergency fund and no debts except for the mortgage, you have control of your finances and need to get serious about your retirement. Be sure to take advantage of any 401K contributions at work. Always deposit the maximum allowed by the Internal Revenue Service in Independent Retirement funds. Your bookkeeper or CPA is a great resource.
5. Create a college fund for children.
   College and higher education costs are growing higher and higher and will sneak up on you. Children tend to grow quickly as time passes by. Start setting aside funds so you will be prepared before high school graduation. Once again, this is an area where your CPA is a great resource for options. There are tax advantage programs for education savings accounts.
6. Pay off your home early.
   Now is the time to take all of your extra money and pay off your home. You should be able to burn the mortgage

in three to five years. You will be saving an enormous amount of money in interest fees.

7. Build wealth, prosperity, and philanthropy.
   This is the last step in taking control of your money and your life. Continue to build wealth and give generously to others and leave inheritances to those you love and care for. Your dreams have come true, and you have been a living example of being the right person, doing the right things, and having all this world has to offer by giving, helping, and serving others. You have created a legacy. An inheritance is leaving material things to people, while a legacy is spiritual and is left inside of them for a lifetime.

FINAL THOUGHTS

Are you saying to yourself, "I do not know how to dream big. I have never done it. What if I look foolish?" Or perhaps you are thinking, "Other people do this, not me. I don't know enough about it. It is too hard and difficult. I'm too old. There is too much competition. Nobody in my family has ever done anything like this."

If this sounds like you, I challenge you to make three decisions that will change your life and your legacy. These three decisions will move your dreams out of your imagination into reality. They will make the impossible possible and the overwhelming as simple as taking one step. They will turn your "I wish" into "I will" and your "I will" into "I did." Something big is in your heart. If you could do it alone, it would not be big enough.

DECISION ONE—TAKE THE FIRST STEP

Go ahead and start. You are meant to do it. Just start! Write th Big God thing down as a goal in your journal. Invest fifteen to twenty minutes each day learning about Your Big God thing.

DECISION TWO—CHOOSE TO LEAVE A LEGACY INTENTIONALLY AND BY DESIGN

Legacy is defined as the things you leave in the heart of those left behind after you are buried. Here are five action items you can take:

1. Create daily legacy moments. Send a text or leave a voicemail. Write a short note and place it in the lunch bag of a child or stick it on the refrigerator door. Always use your most positive legacy words by speaking hope and encouragement.
2. Enjoy a weekly legacy dinner. Rest, relax, and do not rush through the meal. Be intentional about having positive conversations, especially with children. Example: "Johnny, you are a winner, and you make good choices. Continue to study and you will earn a college scholarship." Also, have a discussion centered on the question, "How can we as a family speak to others using our family words of kindness, love, and integrity?"
3. Plan and attend a monthly legacy event. Break the routine. Have a picnic in the park. Take lunch to a neighbor who is isolated and shut in with no way to leave

their house. A demonstration of kindness is better than talking about kindness.

4. Plan and participate in a legacy event each year. Go on a family vacation or attend a family reunion. Go to museums and discuss their significance with the children. Create written documents and take pictures showing the learning experiences. An important legacy question is "What was Grandpa's greatest act of kindness?"

DECISION THREE—CHOOSE TO BEGIN EACH DAY WITH THE "PERFECT START"

Mark Twain once said, "The secret of getting ahead is getting started." This is the most powerful habit in my life. If you choose to do this, every area of your life will change and improve to make you a better you.

Make your life happen to your day—not your day happen to your life. The key is to get your mind working and thinking intentionally about what you need to accomplish each day.

Start small. I invest two hours each day in my "perfect start." I did not begin with two hours each day. I built up to it. Do not try to run a marathon your first time to exercise.

Remove all distractions. I do not check email or look at my phone. I get up early, make the coffee, and get started. The goal is to get your mindset right, then plan your day, and then tackle the objectives.

You must create the time and get up early each day.

I spend time in prayer, meditation, gratitude, reflection, and quiet time talking with God. I read scripture and devotionals, and I read Proverbs each day. In my journal I write my thoug concerns, and my prayer list. I review my daily goals, schedu objectives, and items on my to-do list. I then imagine a menta model of planned face-to-face meetings, telephone calls, and presentations. I decide on the most significant thing for the day that will change all other things. It could be finishing a project, completing a chapter in a book, or working out at a high level of intensity.

All of this takes me approximately two hours. You might not have the time to do this in the beginning, but allow me to suggest a way to get started. It only takes ten minutes.

For three minutes, write down three things you are grateful for … gratitude is the most beneficial habit to choose. Then meditate on the good things going on in your life.

Use the next three minutes to read Proverbs (there are thirty-one proverbs in the Bible, one for each day of the month) or something inspirational and uplifting.

For the last four minutes, write your major goals and a to-do list for the day. Keep the list with you to stay on track during the day. Now it's your turn. Create your own "perfect start." Use mine as an example.

Review your why and purpose, your desires, goals, and dreams. Reflect on the legacy you want to leave behind.

Begin each day with the "perfect start." It will change your life.

ABOUT THE AUTHOR

Kenneth Robert O'Neal is an author, speaker, coach, and founder and owner of Kroneal Coaching and Training located in Kerrville, Texas. He is a Ziglar legacy certified coach and trainer. O'Neal coauthored *Road Trip* with Tom Ziglar in 2021. In addition, O'Neal serves on the board of directors and is the 2021–2022 president of the Morning Rotary Club of Kerrville, Texas. He is a member of the Salvation Army advisory board, a veteran of the United States Air Force, and a former certified public accountant.

ABOUT THE BOOK

Are you seeking ways to be more prosperous? Do you ever wonder how you can be certain your friendships are genuine and meaningful? Do you long for the peace of mind in knowing your life maximizes your potential to best serve God's purpose?

If you answered *yes* to any of these questions, then you are not alone. People throughout the world long for answers to how to be happier, healthier, kinder, and more secure in their relationships with others and themselves.

The Circle of Gumption presents some of the most important pillars of life in a simple format, easily understood when directly applied to the business of living. The nature of man is a lifelong pursuit of purpose and commitment. These pillars work in the application of life. The greatest project on Earth is to build from the inside to outside and develop a well-balanced person who is beneficial to society.

In his book, *The Circle of Gumption*, Kenneth O'Neal provides perceptive responses to these questions and many more as

he shows how maximizing your God-given talents and abili
leads to a successful, well-balanced existence in all areas of li
The Circle of Gumption will be the difference you need to begi
to change your life mentally, spiritually, physically, financially, and professionally by improving the health of your relationships with others and yourself.

By providing insightful examples and discerning wisdom, O'Neal identifies the four pillars that support living a life of gumption in a way that is clear, observant, and relatable for any person to read. *The Circle of Gumption* will give you the tools you need to be the right person and do the right things so you can give to others and create a legacy to last through eternity.

Made in the USA
Coppell, TX
18 July 2022